BINGO

FLY OUT TO SECOND BASE	BUNT	"3 UP 3 DOWN"	SINGLE TO RIGHT FIELD	GROUND OUT TO SHORTSTOP
STRIKEOUT (CALLED)	ERROR	RUNDOWN	DIVING CATCH OUT	INFIELD SINGLE
SINGLE TEAM GETS 15+ HITS	BATTER KNOCKED OFF HIS FEET BY A PITCH	FREE	CATCHER THROWS OUT RUNNER STEALING	DOUBLE
SACRIFICE FLY	STRIKEOUT (SWINGING)	BATTER LOSES HIS BAT	BATTER FLIES OUT IN FOUL TERRITORY	HOME TEAM WINS
UNASSISTED PUT OUT AT THIRD BASE	GROUND OUT TO FIRST BASE	FOUL BALL HITS THE DUGOUT	WILD PITCH	FLY OUT TO FIRST BASE

WAGER: _____

Fun Fact:

The life span of a major league baseball is 5–7 pitches. During a typical game, approximately 70 balls are used.

Sports Quote:

"There are three types of baseball players: those who make it happen, those who watch it happen and those who wonder what happens." – Tommy Lasorda

Baseball Record:

The youngest pitcher in major league baseball history is Joe Nuxhall (1928–2007) who was just 15 years old when he entered a game and pitched 2/3 of an inning for the Cincinnati Reds.

BINGO

INFIELD SINGLE	GROUND OUT TO FIRST BASE	BATTER GETS HIT BY PITCH	UNASSISTED PUT OUT AT THIRD BASE	RUNNER SLIDES INTO FIRST BASE
FLY OUT TO CENTER FIELD	STOLEN BASE (SECOND BASE)	BUNT	SINGLE TEAM SCORES 4+ RUNS	SACRIFICE FLY
STOLEN BASE (SECOND BASE)	DIVING CATCH (OUT)	FREE	HOME RUN	BATTER GROUNDS OUT TO PITCHER
CATHER THROWS OUT RUNNER STEALING	HOME TEAM WINS	PITCHER WALKS BATTER ON 4 STRAIGHT PITCHES	TRIPLE	BATTER FLIES OUT TO CENTER FIELD
RUNDOWN	SINGLE TO LEFT FIELD	"3 UP 3 DOWN"	STRIKEOUT (CALLED)	DOUBLE

WAGER:

Fun Fact:
A "can of corn" is an easy fly ball. The term comes from when old-time grocers used their aprons to catch cans knocked from a high shelf.

Sports Quote:
"The great thing about baseball is there's a crisis every day." – Gabe Paul

Baseball Record:
While Jackie Robinson is commonly thought to be the first African-American baseball player in the big leagues when he played on April 15, 1947, another African-American named William Edward White played a single game for the National League's Providence Grays on June 21, 1879, making him the first.

BINGO

WILD PITCH	UMPIRE CALL OVERTURNED (REPLAY)	FLY OUT TO SHORT STOP	RUNNER TAGS UP	SINGLE TO LEFT FIELD
GROUND RULE DOUBLE	BALL HITS OUTFIELD WALL	TRIPLE	RUNNER SLIDES INTO FIRST BASE	GROUND OUT TO SHORT STOP
HOME TEAM WINS	STRIKEOUT (SWINGING)	FREE	STOLEN BASE (THIRD BASE)	GROUND OUT TO FIRST BASE
BROKEN BAT	GROUND OUT TO CATCHER	UNASSISTED PUT OUT AT THIRD BASE	FLY OUT TO RIGHT FIELD	LINE DRIVE OUT
GROUND OUT TO PITCHER	BATTER LEADS OFF INNING DOUBLE	BATTER HIT BY PITCH	INTENTIONAL WALK	SINGLE TO CENTER FIELD

WAGER:

Fun Fact:

Baseball's L.A. Dodgers, originally founded in Brooklyn, are named after the legendary skill that that local residents showed at "dodging" the city's trolley streetcar system.

Sports Quote:

"There are only five things you can do in baseball — run, throw, catch, hit and hit with power." — Leo Durocher

Baseball Record:

Cal Ripken Jr. holds the record for playing in the most consecutive baseball games. He played in 2,632 games and was twice named the American League's Most Valuable Player, in 1983 and 1991. He didn't miss a game in 16 years.

BINGO

Ground Rule Double	Umpire Gets Hit With Ball	Batter Leads Off Inning Single	Broken Bat	Stolen Base (Third Base)
Sacrifice Fly	Fly Out To Left Field	Ground Out To Shortstop	Batter Strikes Out On 3 Pitches	Ground Out To Third Base
Bunt	Triple	FREE	Double	Home Run
Single To Right Field	Stolen Base (Third Base)	Foul Ball Hits The Dugout	Catcher Throws Out Running Stealing	Batter Leads Off Inning (Double)
Fly Out To First Base	Umpire Walks Ball Out To Pitcher	Batter Hit By Pitch	Intentional Walk	Batter Loses His Bat

WAGER:

Fun Fact:

The baseball team with the most World Series wins is the New York Yankees.

Baseball Quote:

"There are only 3 things you can do in a baseball game: you can win, or you can lose, or it can rain." – Casey Stengel

Baseball Record:

Pete Rose (1941 –) from the Cincinnati Reds holds the all time record for hits (4,256) and games played (3,562). He agreed to a lifetime ban from baseball after he was caught betting on the team he managed multiple times.

BINGO

GROUNDER UP THE MIDDLE (SINGLE)	PITCHING CHANGE	EXTRA INNINGS	WALK ON 4 PITCHES	DOUBLE PLAY
DOUBLE	BUNT	BATTER FLIES OUT IN FOUL TERRITORY	"3 UP 3 DOWN"	BATTER FLIES OUT TO CATCHER
STOLEN BASE (SECOND BASE)	CAUGHT STEALING OR PICK OFF BY PITCHER	FREE	RUNNER TAGS UP	RUNNER SLIDES INTO FIRST BASE
LEAD OF INNING WALK	FOUL BALL HITS THE DUGOUT	BALL HITS OUTFIELD WALL	GROUND OUT TO THIRD BASE	INFIELD SINGLE
HOME RUN	UMPIRE CALL OVERTURNED (REPLAY)	FLY OUT TO SECOND BASE	VISITING TEAM WINS	BATTER HIT BY PITCH

WAGER: _____

Fun Fact:

The first-ever radio broadcast of a major league baseball game occurred on August 5, 1921, by radio station KDKA in Pittsburgh. The first place Pirates beat the last place Philadelphia Phillies 8–5 at Forbes Field. It also featured the game's first live play-by-play announcer, 26-year-old Harold Arlin.

Sports Quote:

"I see great things in baseball. It's our game – the American game." – Walt Whitman

Baseball Record:

Joe DiMaggio has hit in the most consecutive games: 56 in 1941.

BINGO

GROUND OUT TO PITCHER	BLOWN SAVE	TEAM LEAVES 2 RUNNERS ON INNING	RUNNER TAGS UP	BROKEN BAT
STOLEN BASE (SECOND BASE)	UMPIRE WALKS BALL OUT TO PITCHER	INTENTIONAL WALK	BATTER FLIES OUT IN FOUL TERRITORY	DIVING CATCH (OUT)
STOLEN BASE (THIRD BASE)	CAUGHT STEALING OR PICK OFF BY PITCHER	FREE	BALL HITS OUTFIELD WALL	INFIELD SINGLE
STARTING PITCHER TAKEN OUT BEFORE 5TH INNING	BATTER LEADS OFF INNING SINGLE	UNASSISTED PUT OUT AT FIRST BASE	EXTRA INNINGS	DOUBLE
GROUND BALL UP THE MIDDLE (SINGLE)	FLY OUT TO SHORTSTOP	UNASSISTED PUT OUT AT THIRD BASE	BATTER STRIKES OUT ON 3 PITCHES	SINGLE TEAM GETS 10+ HITS

WAGER:

Fun Fact:
In 2008, Dr. David A. Peters found that sliding headfirst into a base is faster than a feet-first slide.

Sports Quote:
"Baseball is more than a game. It's like life played out on a field." – Juliana Hatfield

Baseball Record:
Ty Cobb has the highest career batting average: .3662

BINGO

RUNDOWN	BATTER FLIES OUT TO PITCHER	INTENTIONAL WALK	UNASSISTED DOUBLE PLAY	BATTER FLIES OUT IN FOUL TERRITORY
BATTER LOSES HIS BAT	BUNT	BALL HITS OUTFIELD WALL	BATTER HIT BY PITCH	HOME RUN
SACRIFICE FLY	LEAD OFF INNING HOME RUN	FREE	INFIELD HIT	SINGLE TEAM SCORES 4+ RUNS
DOUBLE	BATTER FLIES OUT TO CATCHER	RUNNER SLIDES INTO FIRST BASE	HOME TEAM WINS	DOUBLE PLAY
GROUND RULE DOUBLE	BATTER LEADS OFF INNING WALK	UNASSISTED PUT OUT AT FIRST BASE	CATCHER THROWS OUT RUNNER STEALING	BATTER HITS SINGLE TO LEFT FIELD

WAGER: _____

Fun Fact:

The New York Yankees were the first baseball team to wear numbers on their backs, in the 1920s. They initially wore numbers based on the batting order. Babe Ruth always hit third, so he was number 3.

Sports Quote:

"Playing baseball for a living is like having a license to steal." – Pete Rose

Baseball Record:

Hank Aaron has the most career runs batted in: 2,297

BINGO

WILD PITCH	VISITING TEAM WINS	FLY OUT TO FIRST BASE	GRAND SLAM	BATTER WALKS ON 4 STRAIGHT PITCHES
ERROR	UMPIRE CALL OVERTURNED (REPLAY)	SINGLE TEAM SCORES 5+ RUNS	DOUBLE PLAY	BLOWN SAVE
GROUND OUT TO CATCHER	INFIELD HIT	FREE	BUNT	TEAM LEAVES 3 RUNNERS ON INNING
SACRIFICE FLY	RUNDOWN	SINGLE TO LEFT FIELD	UNASSISTED PUT OUT AT THIRD BASE	SINGLE TO CENTER FIELD
FLY OUT TO SHORT STOP	DIVING CATCH (OUT)	FLY OUT TO RIGHT FIELD	CATCHER THROWS OUT RUNNING STEALING	GROUND OUT TO SHORT STOP

WAGER: _____

Fun Fact:

Baseball has been called America's national pastime since the Civil War. Indeed, its popularity increased during that war (1861–65) as both Union and Confederate soldiers played the game as a morale booster and emotional escape when they had time.

Sports Quote:

"If my uniform doesn't get dirty, I haven't done anything in the baseball game." – Rickey Henderson

Baseball Record:

Gus Weyhing has hit the most batters: 278

BINGO

Runner Slides Into First Base	Bunt	Single To Left Field	Fly Out To Second Base	Team Leaves 3 Runners On Inning
Single Team Scores 3+ Runs	Batter Walks On 4 Consecutive Pitches	Unassisted Put Out At First Base	Unassisted Double Play	Stolen Base (Second Base)
Called 3rd Strike (Strike Out)	Triple	FREE	Ball Hits Outfield Wall	Visiting Team Wins
Runner Tags Up	Lead Off Inning Double	Home Run	Batter Strikes Out On 3 Pitches	Ground Out To First Base
Fly Out To Left Field	Wild Pitch	Double Play	Pitcher Picks Off Runner	Error

WAGER:

Fun Fact:

The first U.S. president to throw the ceremonial first ball was William Howard Taft (a former semi-pro baseball player) on April 14, 1910. American presidents, except for Jimmy Carter and Donald Trump, have been throwing out the first ball on Opening Day ever since.

Sports Quote:

"Fans don't boo nobodies." – Mr. October, Reggie Jackson

Baseball Record:

Rickey Henderson has the most career runs scored: 2,295

BINGO

DOUBLE PLAY	DIVING CATCH (OUT)	UMPIRE CALL UPHELD (REPLAY)	FLY OUT TO LEFT FIELD	RUNDOWN
GROUND OUT TO THIRD BASE	SACRIFICE FLY	TEAM LEAVES 2 RUNNERS ON INNING	FLY OUT TO FIRST BASE	FLY OUT TO RIGHT FIELD
SINGLE TO LEFT FIELD	SINGLE TEAM GETS 15+ HITS	FREE	INFIELD SINGLE	ERROR
GROUND OUT TO FIRST BASE	STARTING PITCHER TAKEN OUT BEFORE 6TH INNING	"3 UP 3 DOWN"	BATTER FLIES OUT IN FOUL TERRITORY	SINGLE TEAM SCORES 6+ RUNS
GRAND SLAM	SINGLE TO CENTER FIELD	BATTER WALKS ON 4 STRAIGHT PITCHES	WILD PITCH	BATTER LEADS OFF INNING SINGLE

WAGER:

Fun Fact:

George Herman Ruth, Jr. (Babe Ruth) was nicknamed "Babe" when a player saw Baltimore Orioles manager Jack Dunn with his new player and said, "There goes Dunnie with his new babe."

Sports Quote:

"Baseball hasn't forgotten me. I go to a lot of old-timers games and I haven't lost a thing. I sit in the bullpen and let people throw things at me. Just like old times." – Bob Uecker

Baseball Record:

Orel Hershiser has thrown the most consecutive scoreless innings: 59

BINGO

SINGLE TO RIGHT FIELD	BATTER LEADS OFF INNING HOME RUN	FLY OUT TO FIRST BASE	TEAM LEAVES 3 RUNNERS ON INNING	BATTER FLIES OUT TO CENTER FIELD
SINGLE TEAM SCORES 4+ RUNS	SINGLE TEAM GETS 15+ HITS	GROUND OUT TO CATCHER	FAN THROWS HOME RUN BALL BACK	GROUND BALL OR LINE DRIVE UP THE MIDDLE (SINGLE)
RUNDOWN	FLY OUT TO LEFT FIELD	FREE	GROUND OUT TO FIRST BASE	GROUND OUT TO SHORT STOP
BATTER HIT BY PITCH	BATTER LEADS OFF INNING SINGLE	BALL HITS OUTFIELD WALL	CATCHER THROWS OUT RUNNER STEALING	PITCHING CHANGE
ERROR	DOUBLE PLAY	UMPIRE WALKS BALL OUT TO PITCHER	SINGLE TO LEFT FIELD	RUNNER TAGS UP

WAGER: _____

Fun Fact:

Alexander Cartwright (1820-1892) organized the first ever baseball team named the Knickerbocker Baseball Club of New York, named after a New York City fire department. He also helped create the first-ever written rules of baseball in 1845 and was the first to draft the baseball diamond. He is one of several people named the "Father of Baseball."

Sports Quote:

"Baseball is like church. Many attend few understand." – Leo Durocher

Baseball Record:

Reggie Jackson has struck out more times than any other batter in a career: 2,597

BINGO

Stolen Base (Third Base)	"3 Up 3 Down"	Rundown	Runner Slides Into First Base	Bunt
Batter Flies Out In Foul Territory	Sacrifice Fly	Ball Hits Outfield Wall	Fly Out To Left Field	Runner Tags Up
Batter Walks On 4 Straight Pitches	Unassisted Put Out At First Base	FREE	Ground Out To Pitcher	Fly Out To Third Base
Home Team Wins	Ground Out To Third Base	Fly Out To First Base	Strikeout (Swinging)	Ground Out To First Base
Single To Center Field	Triple	Pitcher Picks Off Runner	Ground Out To Short Stop	Single To Right Field

WAGER:

Fun Fact:

Visiting teams wear (at least mostly) gray uniforms so fans can easily distinguish between the visiting team and the home team. The tradition dates back to the late 1800's when traveling teams did not have time to launder their uniforms and consequently, wore gray to hide the dirt.

Sports Quote:

"To me, baseball has always been a reflection of life. Like life, it adjusts. It survives everything." – Willie Stargell

Baseball Record:

Pete Rose has played the most games in a career: 3,562

BINGO

Fly Out To Short Stop	Ground Out To First Base	Ball Hits Outfield Wall	Fly Out To Catcher	Batter Strikes Out On 3 Straight Pitches
Ground Out To Short Stop	Fly Out To Center Field	Infield Single	Batter Hit By Pitch	Stolen Base (Second Base)
Batter Walks On 4 Straight Pitches	Foul Ball Hits The Dugout	FREE	Batter Loses His Bat	Strikeout (Called)
Single To Left Field	Catcher Throws Out Runner Stealing	Batter Leads Off Inning Double	Umpire Called Overturned (Replay)	Home Team Wins
Fly Out To Right Field	"3 Up 3 Down"	Sacrifice Fly	Batter Flies Out In Foul Territory	Ball Hits Outfield Wall

WAGER: _____

Fun Fact:
"Soaking" was a very early baseball rule that allowed a runner who was off base to be put out by throwing a ball at him.

Sports Quote:
"Progress always involves risk. You can't steal second base and keep your foot on first." – Frederick B. Wilcox

Baseball Record:
Cy Young has won the most career games as a pitcher: 511

BINGO

GROUND OUT TO THIRD BASE	ERROR	INFIELD SINGLE	FLY OUT TO LEFT FIELD	"3 UP 3 DOWN"
DOUBLE	UMPIRE GETS HIT WITH BALL	UMPIRE WALKS BALL OUT TO PITCHER	RUNNER SLIDES INTO FIRST BASE	BATTER STRIKES OUT ON 3 STRAIGHT PITCHES
BATTER FLIES OUT TO CATCHER	GROUND BALL UP THE MIDDLE (SINGLE)	FREE	BATTER HIT BY PITCH	FLY OUT TO SECOND BASE
TRIPLE	FAN THROWS HOME RUN BALL BACK	BATTER FLIES OUT IN FOUL TERRITORY	RUNNER TAGS UP	PITCHING CHANGE
BATTER LEADS OFF INNING SINGLE	SINGLE TEAM SCORES 4+ RUNS	FLY OUT TO THIRD BASE	STOLEN BASE (SECOND BASE)	HOME RUN

WAGER: _____

Fun Fact:

A major league baseball must have lacing with exactly 108 stitches. It also must have a circumference between 9.00 and 9.25 inches, a weight between 5.00 and 5.25 ounces, and two pieces of cowhide laced together with red-waxed cotton stitches.

Sports Quote:

"In baseball, you can't kill the clock. You've got to give the other man his chance. That's why this is the greatest game." - Earl Weaver

Baseball Record:

Boston Braves pitcher Red Barrett threw the least amount of pitches ever in a complete game: 58 in 1944.

BINGO

VISITING TEAM WINS	GROUND OUT TO PITCHER	SINGLE TEAM GETS 15+ HITS	GROUND RULE DOUBLE	BALL HITS OUTFIELD WALL
UMPIRE CALL UPHELD (REPLAY)	EXTRA INNINGS	FLY OUT TO CATCHER	SINGLE TEAM SCORES 4+ RUNS	GROUND OUT TO FIRST BASE
STOLEN BASE (SECOND BASE)	UMPIRE WALKS BALL OUT TO PITCHER	FREE	RUNDOWN	BATTER HIT BY PITCH
BATTER LEADS OFF INNING SINGLE	UNASSISTED DOUBLE PLAY	FLY OUT TO SHORT STOP	FLY OUT TO LEFT FIELD	STOLEN BASE (THIRD BASE)
CATHER THROWS OUT RUNNER STEALING	BATTER FLIES OUT IN FOUL TERRITORY	STRIKEOUT (CALLED)	TEAM LEAVES 2 RUNNERS ON INNING	BATTER FLIES OUT TO CATCHER

WAGER:

Fun Fact:

When baseball great Lou Gehrig retired from the game due to amyotrophic lateral sclerosis (ALS), he said in his farewell speech that he was "the luckiest man on the face of the earth." His speech has been called the "Gettysburg Address of Baseball."

Sports Quote:

"You can't be afraid to make errors! You can't be afraid to be naked before the crowd, because no one can ever master the game of baseball, or conquer it. You can only challenge it." – Lou Brock

Baseball Record:

Nolan Ryan has thrown the most no-hitters: 7

BINGO

Single Team Scores 12+ Runs	Batter Fly Out To First Base	Runner Slides Into First Base	Bare Handed Throw Out	Batter Hit By Pitch
Batter Leads Off Inning Home Run	Intentional Walk	Catcher Throws Out Runner Stealing	Strikeout (Called)	Double
Ground Out To Short Stop	Stolen Base (First Base)	FREE	Infield Single	Diving Catch (Out)
Broken Bat	Fly Out To Third Base	"3 Up 3 Down"	Fly Out To Left Field	Ground Ball Up The Middle (Single)
Single Team Gets 10+ Hits	Batter Strikes Out On 3 Straight Pitches	Pitching Change	Batter Loses His Bat	Team Leaves 2 Runners On Inning

WAGER:

Fun Fact:

A baseball catcher's equipment is sometimes called "tools of ignorance" because it is said that catching is such a difficult job that no intelligent person would do it.

Sports Quote:

"That's one of the great gifts of this, the greatest of all games, baseball: it allows you, still, to lose yourself in a dream, to feel and remember a season of life when summer never seemed to die and the assault of cynicism hadn't begun to batter optimism." — Mike Barnicle

Baseball Record:

Yogi Berra of the New York Yankees has the most World Series Championships as a player: 10

BINGO

Stolen Base (Second Base)	Infield Single	Error	Single To Left Field	Diving Catch (Out)
Home Run	Fly Out To Center Field	Fly Out To Short Stop	Ground Out To Third Base	Starting Pitcher Taken Out Of Game Before 5th Inning
Ground Rule Double	Unassisted Double Play	FREE	Fly Out To First Base	Triple
Umpire Call Upheld (Replay)	Extra Innings	Stolen Base (Third Base)	Fly Out To Catcher	Bare Handed Throw Out
Batter Loses His Bat	Runner Slides Into First Base	Batter Leads Off Inning Home Run	Runner Tags Up	Batter Flies Out In Foul Territory

WAGER:

Fun Fact:

The most innings ever played in a Major League Baseball game was 26 innings on May 1, 1920, when the Brooklyn Dodgers played the Boston Braves.

Sports Quote:

"Little League baseball is a very good thing because it keeps the parents off the streets." – Yogi Berra

Baseball Record:

Jesse Orosco has pitched in the most games: 1,252

BINGO

SINGLE TO CENTER FIELD	BATTER LEADS OFF INNING DOUBLE	BALL HITS OUTFIELD WALL	"3 UP 3 DOWN"	GROUND OUT TO CATCHER
BATTER FLIES OUT IN FOUL TERRITORY	UMPIRE CALL UPHELD (REPLAY)	SINGLE TEAM SCORES 4+ RUNS	BATTER HIT BY PITCH	LINE DRIVE OUT
TEAM LEAVES 2 RUNNERS ON INNING	BATTER KNOCKED OFF HIS FEET BY A PITCH	FREE	PITCHER WALKS BATTER ON 4 STRAIGHT PITCHES	PITCHING CHANGE
UMPIRE GETS HIT BY BALL	VISITING TEAM WINS	DOUBLE	SINGLE TEAM GETS 12+ HITS	BARE HANDED THROW OUT
STOLEN BASE (SECOND BASE)	FLY OUT TO SECOND BASE	FLY OUT TO SHORT STOP	WILD PITCH	GRAND SLAM

WAGER: _____

Fun Fact:

In 1919, the Chicago White Sox earned the name "Black Sox" when eight players were accused of intentionally losing the World Series. The eight players were banned from baseball for life, including "Shoeless" Joe Jackson, one of baseball's all-time greatest hitters. Because he was kicked out, he is also ineligible for the Hall of Fame.

Sports Quote:

"You could be a kid for as long as you want when you play baseball." – Cal Ripken, Jr

Baseball Record:

Hughie Jennings (1891–1918) was well respected for his ability to step into a pitch and take one for the team. He is the all time leader in getting hit with a pitch: 287

BINGO

STOLEN BASE (THIRD BASE)	FOUL BALL HITS DUGOUT	SINGLE TEAM SCORES 4+ RUNS	STRIKEOUT (CALLED)	GROUND RULE DOUBLE
CATCHER THROWS OUT RUNNER STEALING	DOUBLE	"3 UP 3 DOWN"	GRAND SLAM	FLY OUT TO SHORT STOP
SACRIFICE FLY	STOLEN BASE (SECOND BASE)	FREE	RUNNER SLIDES INTO FIRST BASE	BATTER FLIES OUT TO THIRD BASE
TRIPLE	BUNT	INFIELD SINGLE	SINGLE TO CENTER FIELD	HOME TEAM WINS
GROUND OUT TO CATCHER	FLY OUT TO CENTER FIELD	BATTER LEADS OFF INNING HOME RUN	GROUND OUT TO PITCHER	RUNNER TAGS UP

WAGER:

Fun Fact:

A pitched ball has killed only one major league player. Ray Chapman of the Cleveland Indians was fatally hit in the head on August 16, 1920, by a ball thrown by Yankee pitcher Carl Mays.

Sports Quote:

"I chose baseball because to me baseball is the best game of all." – Dave Winfield

Baseball Record

Rogers Hornsby has the highest single season batting average: .424 in 1924.

BINGO

Team Leaves 3 Runners On Inning	Infield Hit	Visiting Team Wins	Cather Throws Out Runner Stealing	Runner Picked Off By Pitcher
Ground Out To First Base	Error	Runner Slides Into First Base	Diving Catch (Out)	Runner Tags Up
Double Play	Triple	FREE	Batter Loses His Bat	Single Team Scores 5+ Runs
Batter Flies Out To Catcher	Ground Out To Third Base	Double	Fly Out To Short Stop	Pitching Change
Sacrifice Fly	Broken Bat	Stolen Base (Third Base)	Ground Out To Short Stop	Batter Leads Off Inning Double

WAGER: _____

Fun Fact:

The unofficial anthem of American baseball – "Take Me Out to the Ballgame" – is traditionally sung during the middle of the 7th inning. It was written in 1908 by Jack Norworth and Albert Von Tilzer, both of whom had never been to a baseball game.

Baseball Quote:

"Baseball is ninety percent mental and the other half is physical." – Yogi Berra

Baseball Record:

The shortest player to ever bat in a major league baseball game was Eddie Gaedel (1925–1961), who was 3 feet, 7 inches tall. He came to the plate for the St. Louis Browns against the Detroit Tigers on August 19, 1951, during part of publicity stunt.

BINGO

ERROR	"3 UP 3 DOWN"	BATTER STRIKES OUT ON 3 STRAIGHT PITCHES	UMPIRE WALKS BALL OUT TO PITCHER	BATTER LEADS OFF INNING SINGLE
SINGLE TEAM GETS 15+ HITS	SINGLE TEAM SCORES 6+ RUNS	CATCHER THROWS OUT RUNNER STEALING	BATTER FLIES OUT IN FOUL TERRITORY	UMPIRE GETS HIT WITH BALL
BUNT	INFIELD SINGLE	FREE	FLY OUT TO RIGHT FIELD	FLY OUT TO SHORT STOP
FLY OUT TO FIRST BASE	GROUND OUT TO PITCHER	BATTER HIT BY PITCH	STOLEN BASE (THIRD BASE)	DOUBLE PLAY
VISITING TEAM WINS	FLY OUT TO THIRD BASE	PITCHER PICKS OFF RUNNER	HOME RUN	GROUND RULE DOUBLE

WAGER:

Fun Fact:

The first-ever television broadcast of a major league baseball game was on August 26, 1939, when the Cincinnati Reds played a doubleheader against the Brooklyn Dodgers at Ebbets Field.

Sports Quote:

"Baseball is like driving, it's the one who gets home safely that counts." – Tommy Lasorda

Baseball Record:

Mickey Mantle has hit the most home runs during a career in the World Series: 18

BINGO

"3 UP 3 DOWN"	GROUND RULE DOUBLE	DOUBLE PLAY	WILD PITCH	FLY OUT TO SECOND BASE
PITCHING CHANGE	SINGLE TEAM GETS 12+ HITS	BATTER LEADS OFF INNING WALK	SACRIFICE FLY	TRIPLE
BATTER HIT BY PITCH	DOUBLE	FREE	BALL HITS OUTFIELD WALL	ERROR
GROUND OUT TO THIRD BASE	DIVING CATCH (OUT)	STOLEN BASE (SECOND BASE)	HOME RUN	UMPIRE WALKS BALL OUT TO PITCHER
SINGLE TEAM SCORE 5+ RUNS	FLY OUT IN FOUL TERRITORY	GROUND OUT TO PITCHER	GRAND SLAM	RUNNER SLIDES INTO FIRST BASE

WAGER:

Fun Fact:

"Cranks" was an early term for baseball fans in the late 1880's. The term "fan" is said to be a shortened form of "fanatic."

Sports Quote:

"Baseball is the only field of endeavor where a man can succeed three times out of ten and be considered a good performer." – Ted Williams

Baseball Record:

Barry Bonds has hit the most career home runs: 762

BINGO

STOLEN BASE (THIRD BASE)	STRIKEOUT (SWINGING)	BATTER STRIKES OUT ON 3 STRAIGHT PITCHES	TEAM LEAVES 3 RUNNERS ON INNING	STRIKEOUT (CALLED)
BUNT	FLY OUT TO FIRST BASE	GROUND OUT TO CATCHER	STOLEN BASE (THIRD BASE)	RUNNER SLIDES INTO FIRST BASE
SINGLE TO RIGHT FIELD	GROUND OUT TO FIRST BASE	FREE	SINGLE TEAM SCORES 5+ RUNS	GRAND SLAM
FLY OUT TO SHORT STOP	RUNNER TAGS UP	UNASSISTED PUT OUT AT FIRST BASE	BATTER FLIES OUT TO THIRD BASE	SACRIFICE FLY
GROUND BALL UP THE MIDDLE (SINGLE)	GROUND RULE DOUBLE	CATCHER THROWS OUT RUNNER STEALING	UMPIRE CALL OVERTURNED (REPLAY)	INFIELD SINGLE

WAGER:

Fun Fact:

In 1931, Chattanooga shortstop Johnny Jones was traded to the Charlotte Hornets for a 25-pound turkey. Equally bizarre was when Jack Fenton was traded to San Francisco of the Pacific Coast League for a bag of prunes. The most famous sale in baseball history took place in 1919 when the Yankees paid Boston $125,000 for Babe Ruth.

Sports Quote:

"They give you a round bat, and they throw you a round ball, and then they tell you to hit it square." – Willie Stargell

Baseball Record:

Ed Walsh has the lowest career earned run average: 1.82

BINGO

BATTER GROUNDS OUT TO PITCHER	RUNDOWN	GROUND RULE DOUBLE	BATTER STRIKES OUT ON 3 STRAIGHT PITCHES	BROKEN BAT
STOLEN BASE (THIRD BASE)	FLY OUT TO THIRD BASE	BALL HITS OUTFIELD WALL	BATTER LOSES HIS BAT	SINGLE TO RIGHT FIELD
UMPIRE WALKS BALL OUT TO PITCHER	RUNNER SLIDES INTO FIRST BASE	FREE	SINGLE TEAM GETS 10+ HITS	HOME TEAM WINS
PITCHING CHANGE	SINGLE TO CENTER FIELD	DOUBLE PLAY	RUNNER TAGS UP	BATTER FLIES OUT IN FOUL TERRITORY
STRIKEOUT (CALLED)	INTENTIONAL WALK	TRIPLE	BATTER FLIES OUT TO FIRST BASE	HOME RUN

WAGER:

Fun Fact:

There is a rule in baseball that before every game, an umpire should remove the shine from the new baseballs by rubbing them with mud from a creek in Burlington County, New Jersey.

Sports Quote:

"Every day is a new opportunity. You can build on yesterday's success or put its failures behind and start over again. That's the way life is, with a new game every day, and that's the way baseball is." – Bob Feller

Baseball Record:

Pete Rose has the most career base hits: 4,256

BINGO

WILD PITCH	FLY OUT TO SECOND BASE	FLY OUT TO CENTER FIELD	DOUBLE	BATTER FLIES OUT IN FOUL TERRITORY
LINE DRIVE OUT	BLOWN SAVE	BATTER LOSES HIS BAT	GROUND OUT TO FIRST BASE	UMPIRE CALL OVERTURNED (REPLAY)
FLY OUT TO LEFT FIELD	RUNDOWN	FREE	TEAM LEAVES 2 RUNNERS ON INNING	RUNNER SLIDES INTO FIRST BASE
SACRIFICE FLY	GROUND OUT TO PITCHER	GROUND RULE DOUBLE	BUNT	INFIELD SINGLE
FLY OUT TO THIRD BASE	UMPIRE WALKS BALL OUT TO PITCHER	STRIKEOUT (CALLED)	BALL HITS OUTFIELD WALL	DIVING CATCH (OUT)

WAGER:

Fun Fact:

"The Star-Spangled Banner" was performed for the first time at a sporting event on September 5, 1918, in the middle of the 7th inning of Game 1 of the World Series between the Boston Red Sox and the Chicago Cubs at (rented out) Comiskey Park.

Sports Quote:

"There is no room in baseball for discrimination. It is our national pastime and a game for all." – Lou Gehrig

Baseball Record:

Rickey Henderson has the most career stolen bases: 1,406

BINGO

Strikeout (Swinging)	Sacrifice Fly	Ground Rule Double	Ground Out To First Base	Grand Slam
Bunt	Fly Out To Second Base	Umpire Gets Hit With Ball	Starting Pitcher Taken Out Before 6th Inning	Batter Flies Out In Foul Territory
Stolen Base (Third Base)	Runner Slides Into First Base	FREE	Foul Ball Hits Dugout	"3 Up 3 Down"
Runner Tags Up	Ball Hits Outfield Wall	Batter Leads Off Inning Hitting A Single	Fly Out To Catcher	Broken Bat
Umpire Call Overturned (Replay)	Bare Handed Throw Out	Single Team Has 15+ Hits	Pitcher Walks Batter On 4 Straight Pitches	Ground Out To Short Stop

WAGER:

Fun Fact:

Harry Wright (1835–1895), a former cricket player and businessman, organized the first professional baseball team, the Cincinnati Red Stockings, in 1869. He signed nine players to contracts at an average annual salary of $950. The Red Stockings played their first game on March 15, 1869, against Antioch College, winning 41–7.

Sports Quote:

"A life is not important except in the impact it has on other lives." – Jackie Robinson

Baseball Record:

Hank Aaron has the most total bases: 6,856 (700 more than second place: Stan Musial).

BINGO

INFIELD SINGLE	INTENTIONAL WALK	SINGLE TO LEFT FIELD	DIVING CATCH (OUT)	FLY OUT TO RIGHT FIELD
UMPIRE WALKS BALL OUT TO PITCHER	DOUBLE PLAY	GROUND OUT TO THIRD BASE	FLY OUT TO CATCHER	STOLEN BASE (SECOND BASE)
BATTER STRIKES OUT ON 3 STRAIGHT PITCHES	SINGLE TEAM HAS 15+ TOTAL HITS	FREE	BATTER FLIES OUT TO CATCHER	GROUND OUT TO PITCHER
BATTER LEADS OFF INNING HOME RUN	TEAM LEAVES 2 RUNNERS ON INNING	GROUND OUT TO FIRST BASE	TRIPLE	SINGLE TEAM SCORES 4+ RUNS
STRIKEOUT (CALLED)	WILD PITCH	HOME RUN	"3 UP 3 DOWN"	BUNT

WAGER: _____

Fun Fact:
The fastest game ever played in major league history lasted just 51 minutes on September 28, 1919. The New York Giants defeated the Philadelphia Phillies 6-1 at the Polo Grounds.

Sports Quote:
"Do what you love to do and give it your very best. Whether it's business or baseball, or the theater, or any field. If you don't love what you're doing and you can't give it your best, get out of it. Life is too short. You'll be an old man before you know it." - Al Lopez

Baseball Record:
Nolan Ryan has thrown the most strikeouts: 5,714

BINGO

TRIPLE	BUNT	CATCHER THROWS OUT RUNNER STEALING	SINGLE TEAM SCORES 7+ RUNS	HOME RUN
UNASSISTED PUT OUT AT SECOND BASE	INTENTIONAL WALK	DOUBLE PLAY	ERROR	SINGLE TEAM GETS 10+ HITS
RUNNER TAGS UP	STARTING PITCHER TAKEN OUT BEFORE 6TH INNING	FREE	TEAM LEAVES 2 RUNNERS ON INNING	SINGLE TO CENTER FIELD
BALL HITS OUTFIELD WALL	BATTER LEADS OFF INNING HOME RUN	BATTER FLIES OUT IN FOUL TERRITORY	STOLEN BASE (SECOND BASE)	FLY OUT TO CATCHER
FOUL BALL HITS DUGOUT	FLY OUT TO SECOND BASE	BATTER LEADS OFF INNING DOUBLE	SINGLE TO RIGHT FIELD	FLY OUT TO LEFT FIELD

WAGER: _____

Fun Fact:

In 1943, with the major leagues depleted due to WW II, Chicago Cubs owner Philip Wrigley started a professional women's softball team to attract fan interest. The team eventually switched from playing softball (pitching underhand) to baseball and changed their name to the All-American Girls Baseball League (AAGBL). The AAGBL played their final season in 1954.

Sports Quote:

"Every strike brings me closer to the next home run." – Babe Ruth

Baseball Record:

Pete Rose has made the most outs in a career: 10,328

BINGO

HOME RUN	INFIELD SINGLE	DIVING CATCH (OUT)	BARE HANDED THROW OUT	SACRIFICE FLY
RUNNER TAGS UP	WILD PITCH	GRAND SLAM	STOLEN BASE (SECOND BASE)	BATTER STRIKES OUT ON 3 PITCHES
UNASSISTED PUT OUT AT THIRD BASE	GROUND RULE DOUBLE	FREE	SINGLE TEAM GETS 10+ HITS	BATTER FLIES OUT IN FOUL TERRITORY
SINGLE TEAM SCORES 4+ RUNS	DOUBLE PLAY	GROUND OUT TO THIRD BASE	BATTER HIT BY PITCH	CATCHER THROWS OUT RUNNER STEALING
FLY OUT TO CENTER FIELD	GROUND OUT TO FIRST BASE	SINGLE TO CENTER FIELD	GROUNDER UP THE MIDDLE (SINGLE)	BUNT

WAGER: _____

Fun Fact:

The last major league ballpark to install lights was Chicago's Wrigley Field in 1988. Until then, the Cubs did not have lights and played all their home games in the daytime.

Sports Quote:

"People ask me what I do in winter when there's no baseball. I'll tell you what I do. I stare out the window and wait for spring." – Rogers Hornsby

Baseball Record:

Mickey Mantle holds the record for the longest home run a 565-foot clout hit at Washington DC's old Griffith Stadium on April 17, 1953. As a switch hitter, he was batting right-handed against left-handed pitcher Chuck Stobbs from the Washington Senators.

BINGO

WILD PITCH	TEAM LEAVES 2 RUNNERS ON INNING	CATCHER THROWS OUT RUNNER STEALING	SINGLE TO RIGHT FIELD	DIVING CATCH (OUT)
FLY OUT TO THIRD BASE	STOLEN BASE (THIRD BASE)	SINGLE TEAM GETS 10+ HITS	CALLED 3RD STRIKE (STRIKE OUT)	UMPIRE GETS HIT WITH THE BALL
DOUBLE	SINGLE TO CENTER FIELD	FREE	INTENTIONAL WALK	GROUND OUT TO FIRST BASE
FLY OUT TO RIGHT FIELD	FLY OUT TO SHORT STOP	HOME TEAM WINS	GRAND SLAM	STOLEN BASE (THIRD BASE)
SINGLE TEAM SCORES 5+ RUNS	UMPIRE CALL UPHELD (REPLAY)	UNASSISTED PUT OUT AT FIRST BASE	BUNT	ERROR

WAGER: _____

Fun Fact:

To achieve the crosshatched diamond pattern on a baseball field, rollers on a mower push the grass slightly forward, similar to running a vacuum back and forth on a plush carpet. Blades bent away from the viewer capture more light and appear paler. Grass blades that are bent toward the viewer look darker.

Sports Quote:

"Baseball is like a poker game. Nobody wants to quit when he's losing; nobody wants you to quit when you're ahead." – Jackie Robinson

Baseball Record:

Cy Young has lost the most career games as a pitcher: 316

Made in the USA
Las Vegas, NV
23 April 2021